**INTER**_Actions_

SMALL GROUP SERIES

# The Real You

DISCOVERING YOUR IDENTITY IN CHRIST

INTERActions

SMALL GROUP SERIES

# The Real You

DISCOVERING YOUR IDENTITY IN CHRIST

## BILL HYBELS

### WITH KEVIN & SHERRY HARNEY

WILLOW CREEK

RESOURCES®

*Helping People Become
Fully Devoted to Christ*

ZondervanPublishingHouse
*Grand Rapids, Michigan*

*A Division of* HarperCollins*Publishers*

*The Real You*
Copyright © 1996 by the Willow Creek Association

Requests for information should be addressed to:

📖 ZondervanPublishingHouse
*Grand Rapids, Michigan 49530*

ISBN: 0-310-20682-0

*Zondervan Editors: Jack Kuhatschek and Rachel Boers*
*Willow Creek Editors: Bill Donahue and Mark Mittelberg*
*Interior design by Rick Devon*

*Printed in the United States of America*

96 97 98 99 00 01 02 03 /❖DC/ 10 9 8 7 6 5 4 3

# CONTENTS

Interactions . . . . . . . . . . . . . . . . . . 7

Introduction: Discovering Your Identity in Christ . . 9

**SESSION 1**
Sons and Daughters . . . . . . . . . . . 11

**SESSION 2**
Saints . . . . . . . . . . . . . . . . . . 17

**SESSION 3**
Soldiers . . . . . . . . . . . . . . . . 23

**SESSION 4**
Ambassadors . . . . . . . . . . . . . . 29

**SESSION 5**
Friends . . . . . . . . . . . . . . . . . 35

**SESSION 6**
Managers . . . . . . . . . . . . . . . 41

Leader's Notes . . . . . . . . . . . . . . 47

# INTERACTIONS

In 1992, Willow Creek Community Church, in partnership with Zondervan Publishing House and the Willow Creek Association, released a curriculum for small groups entitled the Walking with God series. In just three years, almost a half million copies of these small group study guides were being used in churches around the world. The phenomenal response to this curriculum affirmed the need for relevant and biblical small group materials.

At the writing of this curriculum, there are over 1,000 small groups meeting regularly within the structure of Willow Creek Community Church. We believe this number will increase as we continue to place a central value on small groups. Many other churches throughout the world are growing in their commitment to small group ministries as well, so the need for resources is increasing.

In response to this great need, the Interactions small group series has been developed. Willow Creek Association and Zondervan Publishing House have joined together to create a whole new approach to small group materials. These eight discussion guides are meant to challenge group members to a deeper level of sharing, to create lines of accountability, to move followers of Christ into action, and to help group members become fully devoted followers of Christ.

## SUGGESTIONS FOR INDIVIDUAL STUDY

1. Begin each session with prayer. Ask God to help you understand the passage and to apply it to your life.
2. A good modern translation, such as the New International Version, the New American Standard Bible, or the New Revised Standard Version, will give you the most help. Questions in this guide are based on the New International Version.
3. Read and reread the passage(s). You must know what the passage says before you can understand what it means and how it applies to you.
4. Write your answers in the spaces provided in the study guide. This will help you to express clearly your understanding of the passage.

5. Keep a Bible dictionary handy. Use it to look up unfamiliar words, names, or places.

## SUGGESTIONS FOR GROUP STUDY

1. Come to the session prepared. Careful preparation will greatly enrich your time in group discussion.
2. Be willing to join in the discussion. The leader of the group will not be lecturing, but will encourage people to discuss what they have learned in the passage. Plan to share what God has taught you in your individual study.
3. Stick to the passage being studied. Base your answers on the verses being discussed rather than on outside authorities such as commentaries or your favorite author or speaker.
4. Try to be sensitive to the other members of the group. Listen attentively when they speak, and be affirming whenever you can. This will encourage more hesitant members of the group to participate.
5. Be careful not to dominate the discussion. By all means participate! But allow others to have equal time.
6. If you are the discussion leader, you will find additional suggestions and helpful ideas in the leader's notes.

## ADDITIONAL RESOURCES AND TEACHING MATERIALS

At the end of this study guide you will find a collection of resources and teaching materials to help you in your growth as a follower of Christ. You will also find resources that will help your church develop and build fully devoted followers of Christ.

# Introduction: Discovering Your Identity in Christ

Picture yourself at a wedding ceremony. Remember hearing the pastor say those famous words, "I now pronounce you husband and wife"? If you were bride or groom you probably had an instant identity crisis. The pastor said you were married, but you didn't really feel any different. As hard as you may have tried, it seemed like you were the same person you were before you said "I do."

It's impossible for two people, at the moment they are united in marriage, to think and feel and act in accordance with their new legal identity. It takes weeks, months, even years before they are living, acting, and feeling married. Identities don't just change overnight.

The same is true of an eighteen-year-old Army recruit who shows up for his first day at boot camp. He's issued a uniform, some boots, a mess kit, a rifle, and he takes an oath. Right away the drill sergeant starts to call him "Soldier!" He doesn't think, feel, or act like one . . . yet. But after basic training and a year of combat duty, that recruit thinks, feels, and acts like the soldier he is. He has appropriated his new identity. It's become a part of him.

What happens with newlyweds and new recruits also happens when a person decides to become a Christ follower. When you repent of personal sin and trust Christ as Savior, the Bible makes the statement that you are now a whole new creation. You may not feel much different. You might feel a whole lot like you did ten minutes before conversion. But over time, you learn how to be like Christ and how God views you. As the months and years pass, you understand this new identity, and begin to think and feel and act accordingly.

In Ephesians 2:4–5 the apostle Paul writes, "But because of his great love for us, God, who is rich in mercy, made us alive with Christ even when we were dead in transgressions—it is by grace you have been saved." This passage says you used to be dead in your trespasses and sin, but now you are made alive with Christ. You used to be unresponsive to the things of

God. You were bored with church, estranged from God. You had a little agreement: He would mind His business, and you would mind yours. Remember those days? You were spiritually dead, lost and confused. But now, because of Christ, you are alive.

In this same chapter Paul says, "But now in Christ Jesus you who once were far away have been brought near through the blood of Christ" (v. 13).

God used to seem so distant to you. He was a stranger. But you don't feel that way any more. Now you feel closer to the God who paid your sin debt with the blood of His Son. Your whole position and attitude have changed.

In verse nineteen we read, "Consequently, you are no longer foreigners and aliens, but fellow citizens with God's people and members of God's household." At one time your identity was that of a stranger and alien to God and His kingdom. But now you are fellow citizens. Saints. Part of God's own household. That's your new identity. Nevertheless, God has declared these things so. In these six interactions we will engage our minds and hearts with this truth.

Excited about your new identity? Well, we haven't even scratched the surface yet. The Bible is filled with descriptions of who you are now that you are a Christ follower. You are His workmanship, an ambassador (that's right—you have a mission), and a friend. It doesn't stop there. God also sees you as a soldier going head-to-head with the forces of evil. And, to top it off, He calls you a saint.

So, get ready to receive the new identification card God has issued you. What a difference it will make in your life! My prayer for you as you begin this study is that you will discover, appropriate, and walk in your new identity in Christ.

*Bill Hybels*

# SONS AND DAUGHTERS

## THE BIG PICTURE

Several years ago I attended a worship gathering where individuals were being encouraged, as the Spirit of God led them, to stand and describe the activity of God in their lives. A young woman stood and said, "I grew up in a home where I really can say, sadly, that I never knew or found out what it was like to be the daughter of a loving father." She said, "I thought I was just destined to live that way, fatherless. But then at a certain age I received Christ and I found out that I have a loving, trustworthy, tender, understanding, always faithful, heavenly Father."

The rest of us who were listening could tell by the sincerity and the tone of her voice that she wasn't referring abstractly to a cold theological doctrine called adoption. She was thinking and feeling and acting in accordance with the identity God had given her. She had learned from the Word of God that she had a Father in heaven who loved her more than words could describe. God had said to her by His Spirit, "You're my daughter. You've got a Father now." And she not only believed it, she felt it. She was moved by it. It changed her forever.

## A WIDE ANGLE VIEW

1   What images and impressions come to mind when you think of your earthly father?

*Some happy times as
a child - sadness
growing up*

*What was one way you experienced the love of your heavenly Father through your earthly father?*

*Complete this sentence: "One way I would have liked to receive love from my dad was . . ."*

Just really getting to know him

## A BIBLICAL PORTRAIT

Read John 1:12; Galatians 4:4–7; and 1 John 3:1

2 What do these passages teach you about your relationship to the Father?

## SHARPENING THE FOCUS

Read Snapshot "The Father's Adoption"

### THE FATHER'S ADOPTION

To my knowledge, the understanding of God as a seeking, intimate, and loving Father is unique to the Christian faith. I'm not aware of any major world religion that has any parallel understanding. It seems in most world religions a person learns doctrines, obeys rules, jumps through the required hoops, serves in a prescribed way, and then is promised a euphoric existence in some far away place. It's all rather cold.

But in biblical Christianity, things are different. God doesn't just save us. He doesn't just justify us and regenerate us by His Holy Spirit and then assign us a condominium somewhere in the cosmos when we die. He saves us, cleanses us, justifies us through the death and sacrifice of Jesus Christ, His Son. Then because of who He is, He claims us and adopts us. He says, "I'm going to make you My son or daughter. You're going to be Mine forever." And then He treats us like sons and daughters: respectfully, tenderly, faithfully, and lovingly. It's amazing, isn't it?

# 3

Since we have been adopted as sons and daughters of God, how should we view our relationship with Him and with other followers of Christ?

*How do you respond to God saying, "You're Mine forever"?*

# 4

Sometimes we feel like outcasts and unworthy of God's love. What causes us to feel this way?

Read Snapshot "The Father's Affection"

---

## THE FATHER'S AFFECTION

In John 5:20, Jesus very casually says, "The Father loves the Son." Jesus didn't have to embellish these words. He lived in the awareness that His Father had a great, great affection for Him, so He felt loved, protected, watched over, nurtured, and provided for. He was full of worship for His Father. He felt free to pray to the Father because all good fathers have a listening ear to their sons and daughters.

Putting it simply, because Jesus felt the Father's love, He thought and behaved and felt like a son. When He taught the Lord's Prayer, He said, "You know how I want all of you to start your prayers? 'Our Father.'" And because we too are His sons and daughters, we should call Him "Father."

Is God your Father? Do you understand that you have been accepted by Him? Do you know you are His beloved child? Psalm 103:13 says, "As a father has compassion on his children, so the LORD has compassion on those who fear him." Do you realize how safe you are because you're His child? How secure?

---

## 5

How have you felt God's fatherly love?

## 6

Who is one person in your life who needs to experience the Father's love right now?

*What can you do in the coming days to share the Father's love with that person?*

Read Snapshot "The Father's Authority"

### THE FATHER'S AUTHORITY

Not only did Jesus live in constant awareness of the Father's affection for Him, but He lived under the Father's authority. Jesus wasn't worried about the Father's authority being destructive or manipulative or negative. You see, when you are absolutely convinced of the Father's affection for you, you have no fear whatsoever of the Father's authority. Because you know He has your best interests in mind, you can be assured that His wisdom, His counsel, and His guidance can be trusted. You find yourself wanting to cooperate and enthusiastically seek ways to bring your life under God's authority.

## 7

When you hear the word "authority," what images come to mind?

*What specific things can the members of your group do to help you grow in submission to the Father's will in your life?*

8 What is one specific area in which you struggle to keep under the authority of your heavenly Father?

*Describe a situation in which someone exercised loving, caring, constructive authority in your life.*

9 Since we are sons and daughters of God, then we have also become brothers and sisters in Christ. What can you do to express genuine family love to other followers of Christ:

- In your small group

- In your home

- In your church

- Among Christians around your community, the nation, and the world

### SAYING THANK YOU

Sometime in the coming week, pick up the phone and call someone who has made a profound impact on your growth as a follower of Christ. Maybe it was your mom or dad or a grandparent or teacher or friend or partner or coworker. If they helped you understand the love and care of your heavenly Father, express your appreciation and love. Thank them for giving you a life-giving understanding of God as your heavenly Father.

### DEAR FATHER

Write a letter to your heavenly Father, telling Him three things. First, thank Him for choosing to adopt you as His child. Next, express your gratitude for the depth of His tender affection for you. Finally, tell Him you will submit to His authority in your life because you know He has your best interests in mind.

# SAINTS

## REFLECTIONS FROM SESSION 1

1. Tell the group what happened when you contacted someone who has impacted your life as a follower of Christ.
2. What did you experience as you wrote a letter to your heavenly Father and expressed your love and submission to His authority? Would you be willing to read a little of the letter you wrote to your heavenly Father to the group?

## THE BIG PICTURE

Once, while preaching a series on our new identity in Christ, a guy who attends our church stopped me and said, "God can call me His son if He wants to, and He can call my wife His daughter, but one thing's for sure, my wife ain't a saint, and neither am I. So if God calls either one of us saints, we need a very thorough explanation of what that whole thing is all about." I could understand this man's dilemma, and I bet you can too.

We've all seen pictures of saints. They look blushingly beautiful in their long, flowing robes, shining halos, and cherub-like smiles. And not only do they look a bit unusual, but if you have ever taken the time to read the stories of their lives, you know that their lives could hardly be called mainstream. Many of the famous saints took poverty oaths. Many of them endured horrendous hardships, having lived in unspeakable conditions in order to try to honor God.

But Paul, interestingly, doesn't apologize for calling all Christians saints. In fact, he uses the term interchangeably with words that refer to all believers. I'm convinced that if the apostle Paul were here in the flesh today he would address all Christians by saying, "I, Paul, a bond servant of the Lord Jesus Christ, greet you, the saints of God." And we would all blush.

## A WIDE ANGLE VIEW

**1** What images come to mind when you hear the word "saint"?

**2** Picture somebody you know who qualifies as a saint. Why do they fit the description?

## A BIBLICAL PORTRAIT

Read Ephesians 1:1, 18; 2:19; 3:8; 4:11–13; 5:3; and 6:18

**3** What do you learn about Paul's view of sainthood in these passages?

*Was there anything in the passages you read that surprised you?*

## SHARPENING THE FOCUS

Read Snapshot "Your Position as a Saint"

### YOUR POSITION AS A SAINT

The Bible teaches that all true believers are saints positionally. Now, let me explain what that means. The moment you trust Christ, confess your sin, and repent of it, something dramatic happens to your spiritual position. The Bible says you were dead. That's rather graphic, isn't it? But now your position has changed from a dead, lifeless corpse to one that is fully alive. Your geographic position, figuratively speaking, changed. You were far off, but now you're brought near. You were strangers, and now you're sons and daughters. You were aliens, and now you're citizens. You were lost and now you're found. These expressions and a host of others like them denote that at the moment of your conversion, your position before God changed. You have been set apart. You're a saint positionally.

**4** If someone called you a saint, how would you respond?

*Why do we have a hard time seeing ourselves as saints?*

*The term "saint" means to be set apart. What does it mean in your life to be set apart for God?*

**5** What can you do to express your appreciation to God for making you a saint?

Read Snapshot "The Life of a Saint"

## THE LIFE OF A SAINT

 I know people who forecast all kinds of nightmares when they think about bringing their behavior into conformity with the Word of God. But, do you know what? It's really not like that. God doesn't want a whole bunch of people who all look alike. He wants your unique personality to be developed, explored, matured, refined, liberated, trained, and then plugged into useful service. He wants every ounce of potential that He's put in you to be actualized. He wants fulfillment to spill over in your soul. He wants to satisfy you. And so He says, "I'll give you the power of My Holy Spirit. I'll give you the guidance from My Word. I'll give you the encouragement and accountability of brothers and sisters. Just have your goal be to live as the Holy Spirit directs you, in alignment with your position in Christ. You are a saint positionally, now act accordingly as you are growing up in Christ."

 What are some of the attitudes and actions that should mark our lives as God's saints:

- In our homes

- In the marketplace

- In our neighborhoods

- In our interaction with seekers

**7** How should we respond when we fall short of God's desire and standards for us as saints?

*How should we respond to others when they fall short?*

## PUTTING YOURSELF IN THE PICTURE

### A CHALLENGE FOR GROWTH

Take time this week to identify one area in your life that does not reflect your status and position as a saint. Once you have identified this area, walk through the process below:

1. Confess your struggles in this area to Jesus and seek forgiveness (read 1 John 1:9).
2. Pray for the power of the Spirit to fill and strengthen you in this area.
3. Set specific goals which will help you resist falling into this area of sin in the future.
4. Ask another follower of Christ to pray for you and keep you accountable in this new area of growth.
5. Acknowledge that your position as a saint is not based on how good you live your life day by day; it is based on the finished work of Jesus Christ on the cross. Ask God to give you strength to keep growing into this new identity.

### A COMMITMENT TO JOURNALING

Take time in the coming week to journal and write your prayers. This may be new for you, but give it your best shot. Just put your heartfelt thoughts and feelings on paper. Focus specifically on your position as a saint. See if you can spend more time thanking God for making you a saint than you do focusing on how you fall short of "sainthood." The more you thank God for your status and position as a saint, the more you will experience a desire to live out this new identity.

# SOLDIERS

## REFLECTIONS FROM SESSION 2

1. How has God deepened your understanding of your position as a saint?
2. How did your experience of journaling and writing your prayers over the past days help you communicate and express your heart to God?

## THE BIG PICTURE

At the Sunday school in which I grew up, the song "Onward Christian Soldiers" was always one of the top ten requested music numbers. I can still hear the tune and the words ringing in my ears, "Onward Christian soldiers, marching as to war, with the cross of Jesus going on before," verse after verse. I didn't have the faintest idea what guerilla warfare had to do with Christianity or Sunday school, but oh, how we loved to sing that song. We would stomp our feet and stab each other with pencils.

Now, years later, I'm beginning to appreciate the theme of that song more and more. You see, the song says that Christians should think of themselves as soldiers in God's army, marching together, moving together, fighting in unison, to defeat satanic forces. It suggests that there's a spiritual war going on between God and the Evil One. When we become Christians, we become sons and daughters, and we become saints, but there is another important identity we take on ourselves. We are automatically enlisted into God's army, and we begin a lifelong term of service under God's command.

The Bible teaches that part of our real identity as Christians is that of being a soldier. We are to be trained, equipped, fit, courageous, confident, Spirit-energized soldiers in the army of God. Not soldiers who are simply defending against the attacks of Satan, but soldiers who are strategizing ways to capture enemy territory. Soldiers who have their hearts set on overcoming the enemy, no matter what the cost.

23

## A WIDE ANGLE VIEW

**1** What are some of the responsibilities of a soldier in the military?

*What qualities would you look for in a good soldier?*

## A BIBLICAL PORTRAIT

Read Ephesians 6:10–18

**2** How is a Christian like a soldier?

*What is some of the military language used in the Bible and by followers of Christ?*

## SHARPENING THE FOCUS

Read Snapshot "Weekend Warriors"

### WEEKEND WARRIORS

God calls us to be ready for battle. Ephesians 6:10–18 reminds us of the need to be prepared for the spiritual battles that will face every follower of Christ. We need to wear our defensive armor as well as know the weapons we can use to fight battles against Satan and his demonic workers. We are called to be ever on our guard and always ready for battle.

However, some of God's soldiers see their call as a weekend diversion. They put on their uniform once a week and play soldier for a Sunday morning. I call these people "weekend warriors." They don't mind spending a little time once a week for the cause, but they don't want their faith to get in the way of their other weekly activities. These people don't want to pay the price to become fully devoted followers of Jesus. They're content to play soldier for a few hours a week and leave the real battles to others.

**3** How do weekend warriors affect the life of the church?

*What impact do they have on the world around them?*

**4** Why would anyone choose to be a weekend warrior?

*What can we do to move weekend warriors back into the battlefield where Jesus wants them to be?*

Read Snapshot "Soldiers Gone AWOL"

## SOLDIERS GONE AWOL

If you tell weak, half-hearted believers that hardships will cause heartache, headaches, and hassles, you may see many go AWOL. However, Paul takes his chances. He says, "Let's just let the truth be known. Soldiers will face suffering. This is war. The stakes are sky high. We're fighting over the destiny of human beings who matter to God."

Jesus, our leader, willingly bled to death to gain the ultimate victory over the Enemy, and He expects us to pay a price for the victories that we gain over the Evil One as well. Because the battle is real, many soldiers have gone AWOL. They have run for the hills, tucked their tails, and turned from the battle. While the battle rages, they sit back in safe territory and avoid any conflict or confrontations. While the ministries of the church suffer, they sit at home and make sure they can keep up with their favorite TV show. While people are dying and going to hell, they are content to stay in their comfort zone and protect their own back. The fact is, there are too many AWOL soldiers in God's army.

**5** Why are there so many AWOL soldiers in the church?

*Were you ever AWOL as a Christian? If so, what caused you to run from the battle?*

**6** How do you feel when you see AWOL Christian soldiers?

*What can we do to get these soldiers back on the front lines?*

Read Snapshot "'Just Say The Word' Soldiers"

---

### "JUST SAY THE WORD" SOLDIERS

One exercise that I work through when I'm taking spiritual inventory of my life is to ask myself what kind of soldier I really am. I ask myself whether I am a weekend warrior or if I've gone AWOL in any way. I try to be brutally honest with myself and God. I encourage you to do the same.

My heart's desire is to be a "Just Say The Word" soldier. I want to be ready for battle at any moment. I want my life to be completely submitted to the Commander in Chief of my soul. It is interesting to note that in the days of Jesus, the word for "Sir" and "Lord" were identical. When we say "Yes, Sir" to Jesus, we are really saying "Yes, Lord." We are acknowledging our submission to our Commander. He says "Jump," we say, " How high?" He says, "Move," and we move. That's what it means to be a "Just Say The Word" soldier. We follow no matter what the cost.

I want to tell you, God honors "Just Say The Word" soldiers. God uses them. He blesses them. God does miracles in their lives. But God won't honor or use or bless unsubmitted soldiers. And it's tough to build an army that's a threat to anybody if it's made up of weekend warriors and AWOL soldiers.

---

## 7

Who are a few "Just Say The Word" soldiers you have known?

*What kinds of characteristics have marked their lives?*

## 8

What are some of the rewards of being a "Just Say The Word" soldier?

*What are some of the costs?*

## 9

Find a partner and discuss what can you do to be more effective as a "Just Say The Word" soldier.

**10** What are some of the battles you are fighting right now

- As a church

- In your family or home

- In the marketplace

- In your community

*What can other soldiers around you do to help you win these battles?*

## PUTTING YOURSELF IN THE PICTURE

### HONEST EVALUATION

Take time this week to honestly reflect on what kind of soldier you are. Think about the three kinds of soldiers presented in this study. Honestly identify where you might have characteristics and practices of each in your life.

### FOR THE BOLD AND COURAGEOUS

After you have identified characteristics and practices of each kind of soldier in your life, thank God for the areas you are a "Just Say The Word" soldier. Thank Him for the strength and victory you are experiencing, and pray for continued power to march forward as a committed soldier in the Lord's army.

Second, in the areas you see yourself as a weekend warrior or an AWOL soldier, confess these to the Commander and Chief of your soul. Ask Jesus to forgive you and to give you strength to submit these areas of your life to Him. Surrender each area to God's control.

Third, if you have allowed a friend to help you in this evaluation process, have them pray for you, support you, and keep you accountable as you seek to live as a "Just Say The Word" Christian every day.

# AMBASSADORS

## REFLECTIONS FROM SESSION 3

1. What is one area you identified as needing to be strengthened as a soldier? What have you done since your last session to grow in this area?
2. What is one spiritual victory you have experienced in recent days?

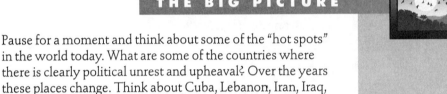

## THE BIG PICTURE

Pause for a moment and think about some of the "hot spots" in the world today. What are some of the countries where there is clearly political unrest and upheaval? Over the years these places change. Think about Cuba, Lebanon, Iran, Iraq, Russia, Bosnia. And the list goes on. Just open your morning paper and you can read about the latest place of conflict.

If you were going to send a representative from your country to a nation in turmoil, you would want just the right ambassador to represent you. If you were the president of our country, what are some of the qualities you would insist on seeing in the life of a potential ambassador to a war-torn nation?

The fact is, an ambassador plays a key role in any reconciliation attempt. He or she can make it or break it. Lots of highly explosive eggs are placed in that person's basket. You can't have an ambassador who is just a nice person, who tiptoes around tough situations and smiles a lot. But neither can you have an ambassador who is too pushy and demanding. You know, one who annoys and offends people with aggressiveness and an overzealous time line for reconciliation. Put another way, you can't afford to have an anonymous ambassador or an obnoxious one. What we're looking for is an effective ambassador. One who does what it takes over time to bring about reconciliation.

## A WIDE ANGLE VIEW

**1** If you had to write a want ad to find an effective ambassador and you only had the space provided below, how would your want ad read?

Desperately seeking an ambassador who . . .

## A BIBLICAL PORTRAIT

Read 2 Corinthians 5:16–20

**2** You are Christ's ambassadors entrusted with the ministry of reconciliation. How does this aspect of your new identity in Christ alter the way you look at the world around you and your role in it?

## SHARPENING THE FOCUS

Read Snapshot "The Anonymous Ambassador"

### THE ANONYMOUS AMBASSADOR

Many believers could be called anonymous kingdom ambassadors. They don't harm the cause of Christ much, but they don't help it much either. Anonymous ambassadors spend time primarily with other embassy employees. They seldom mix with the regular citizens. They feel uncomfortable around the people of the land because they seem crude, speak a different language, have distasteful customs, and hold to different values. The truth is, they prefer to stay in the warmth and familiar setting of the embassy.

## 3

What are some of the dangers and possible consequences of having an apathetic and anonymous ambassador in a tough political situation?

*What are the dangers of having this kind of ambassador representing God in today's world?*

Read Snapshot "The Obnoxious Ambassador"

---

### THE OBNOXIOUS AMBASSADOR

If we are honest, we have to admit there are many Christians who could be called obnoxious kingdom ambassadors—loose cannons firing like it's the Fourth of July. Ambassadors who are gung ho about reconciliation, but they don't nurture it ... they demand it! They're not really interested in getting close to people, being involved in their lives, loving them, resolving doubts, and working through conflicts. They'd rather stand in the public square, blaring out reconciliation plans over loudspeakers, and then castigate the masses for not being more responsive to an offer they can't even fully understand because it was communicated so poorly.

---

## 4

What are some of the possible consequences and dangers of having an obnoxious ambassador representing God in today's world?

*Pause for a moment and put yourself in the shoes of a spiritual seeker who has just met an obnoxious ambassador. How would you feel about that ambassador and his message?*

Read Snapshot "An Effective Ambassador"

---

## AN EFFECTIVE AMBASSADOR

Anonymous ambassadors are oblivious to Spirit-orchestrated opportunities to mark the lives of unbelievers. They're not praying for opportunities to mix with citizens. They're not looking for those opportunities. They're hiding out, staying out of the flow. Obnoxious ambassadors barge into private areas with or without being led by the Spirit. Occasionally they do some good. But often they do more harm.

Effective kingdom ambassadors, however, pray for Spirit-led opportunities. They long to be able to discern an opportunity when it comes their way. These ambassadors ask for divine wisdom when they think an opportunity is coming. They say, "Lord, is this it? What shall I say? What should I do? Holy Spirit, take control this moment. Make me an effective kingdom ambassador.

---

## 5
What are some possible results in the lives of lost people when you act as an effective ambassador?

*Who are some effective kingdom ambassadors you have known and what made them effective?*

## 6
Why is wisdom so important in the life of an effective ambassador?

*What are some ways your group members can work together to develop wisdom in each other's lives?*

**7** What does it mean to be winsome in your witness?

*How can you develop this trait in your life?*

**8** We would all agree that a good ambassador should have a growing knowledge of the Bible and the basics of the faith. To build bridges with lost people, what else must we be knowledgeable about?

**9** What are some of the prevailing values in our culture to be aware of as you live as ambassadors of God's kingdom?

**10** Communication skills are essential for kingdom ambassadors. What can you do to develop your ability to share your faith?

# 11

What practical things can you do to build bridges of reconciliation with the following groups of people?

- Neighbors

- Colleagues at work

- Social acquaintances

- Family members

- Those who consider themselves your enemies

## PUTTING YOURSELF IN THE PICTURE

### PEOPLE AND PLACES

Take time to think about those people God has placed in your life who have not yet been reconciled to Him. In the coming days, pray for each one by name. Ask the Holy Spirit to perform His convicting and mind-opening work. Pray for God's love and a desire for reconciliation to touch their hearts and lives. Also, ask God for a boldness when you sense opportunities to be an ambassador of Christ to these people.

Identify the specific places God puts you in as His ambassador. Pray for a heart filled with God's love and a hunger for reconciling estranged seekers to their Father as you approach each place you go in the coming week.

### A COMMITMENT TO MEMORIZE SCRIPTURE

*We are therefore Christ's ambassadors, as though God were making his appeal through us. We implore you on Christ's behalf: Be reconciled to God (2 Cor. 5:20).*

# FRIENDS

REFLECTIONS FROM SESSION 4

1. Who is one seeker you are praying for at this time? How have you seen God working in their life to draw them to Jesus?
2. What is one place you go where you desire to have an impact for Christ? What are you doing to establish contacts and relationships in this place? How can your group members encourage you in your efforts to be an ambassador?

## THE BIG PICTURE

I had a boss once who was a real slave driver. He used to come right up to my face and with a very loud, booming voice say to me, "Who signs your check? Who? Who?" He sounded like an owl. And I would say, "You do." And then he would say, "So if I asked you to stand on your head in the corner, what do I expect you to do?" I'd say, "Uh, stand on my head in the corner?" He drove me crazy. He was no friend of mine. He was a taskmaster, a slave driver. Leaders like that drain the joy out of work and service. Taskmasters build walls between themselves and others. They rob workers of their dignity.

Jesus said to His followers, "I will never treat you like that. I may be your Commanding Officer, and you're My soldiers, but I will never treat you like a slave owner or a taskmaster. My authority will always have a thread of friendship woven through it. I will respect you. I will treat you with dignity and love."

In this session we're looking at the place where Jesus announces one dimension of our new identities when He says, "I want you to all know that when I look at you as My followers, I see you as being My friends, My personal, close, trusted friends."

## A WIDE ANGLE VIEW

**1** What qualities do you look for in a good friend?

**2** Describe one fond memory of an experience with a friend. (This could be recent or one from the past.)

## A BIBLICAL PORTRAIT

Read John 15:9–17

**3** According to John, how does Jesus show His friendship to us?

*How can we show our love and friendship to Jesus?*

4 In the last few weeks how has Jesus demonstrated His love and friendship to you?

Read Snapshot "Increased Time Together"

## INCREASED TIME TOGETHER

If I were to ask you how you would improve a relationship with an earthly friend, some of you would readily provide some clear answers. You'll find that some of the ways we improve our friendship with Jesus run on parallel paths to the ways we would improve earthly relationships. The first suggestion I want to make to you is an obvious one. Isn't it generally understood that a sure way to improve a relationship is to increase the quantity and quality of time that the individuals spend together? The same is true in our friendship with Jesus.

5 What can you do to increase the quantity and quality of time you spend with Jesus?

Read Snapshot "Removing Barriers"

## REMOVING BARRIERS

The second thing you can do to improve a relationship with a friend, or with Jesus, is to remove any barriers that obstruct the relationship. I suggest you do that through honest communication. Deep, intimate earthly relationships don't develop easily or automatically. Usually, as the friendship deepens there are some tough issues that must be faced. Situations arise that threaten the future of the relationship. Idiosyncrasies come to the surface and you say, "uh-oh, we're going to have to get past this if this relationship is going to grow." There can also be differences in values or opinions. Whatever forms they take, most relationships have barriers that need to be dealt with. In the same way, there are sins, attitudes, and issues that can become barriers between us and Jesus. We need to identify these and remove them.

**6** What are some of the barriers that remain between you and Jesus? How can you remove them?

Read Snapshot "Serving Jesus"

### SERVING JESUS

A third way you can improve your relationship with a friend or with Jesus is to serve them. You know as strange or paradoxical as this sounds, the more you invest in a relationship, the more precious the relationship becomes to you. You might think that if someone serves you they'll become more precious to you. Well, it works the opposite way too. The more you serve somebody, the greater the investment you make in someone's life, the more precious that person becomes to you. Jesus has deepened His relationship with you through service and care. You can deepen your side of the relationship through service as well.

**7** What are you doing in your life right now to serve Jesus?

*How can you enlarge your "servant's heart" toward Jesus?*

Read Snapshot "Saying 'I Love You!'"

### SAYING "I LOVE YOU!"

The fourth way you can improve a relationship with a friend—or with Jesus—is to affirm the importance of the relationship. As corny and antiquated as it sounds, verbal affirmation of the value of a relationship goes a long way in deepening the relationship itself. And, simply put, saying "I love you" helps deepen your relationship with Jesus. Say it often, say it in different ways, but be sure to tell Jesus you love Him.

# 8

If Jesus could tell you how He wants you to love Him, what would He say?

*How would you respond to His request?*

## PUTTING YOURSELF IN THE PICTURE

### MAKING TIME FOR JESUS

You have discussed how important it is to spend time with Jesus. This time with Him will help deepen and develop your friendship. Look at the coming week and schedule specific time to be with Him. Make this as much a priority as anything else in your schedule. If you keep a personal planner, write your time with Jesus in among the other appointments or responsibilities in your day. You might feel a need to commit time every day or maybe three or four times in the coming week. Be realistic with your schedule, but also seek to grow in your commitment to be with Jesus. If you are going to grow as a fully devoted follower of Christ, time with Him is essential.

### A COMMITMENT TO MEMORIZE SCRIPTURE

*Greater love has no one than this, that he lay down his life for his friends (John 15:13).*

# MANAGERS

## REFLECTIONS FROM SESSION 5

1. Were you able to keep your schedule with Jesus over the past days? If you are doing well, what has helped you develop discipline in keeping your friendship with Jesus a priority in your life? If you have been struggling, what has kept you from spending time with the Savior?
2. What can your group members do to help encourage and support you in spending time with Jesus in the coming weeks?

## THE BIG PICTURE

Several of Jesus' most colorful parables were about stewards or managers. He talked about managers who were effective and careful and others who were unjust and careless. The apostle Paul called himself a manager of God's truth. He also encouraged other believers to view themselves as managers. The apostle Peter encouraged all believers to use their spiritual gifts in service to one another. In so doing, they would be good managers of God's grace. Jesus took it for granted that all of His followers viewed themselves as managers. He asked the following question rather pensively: "Who will be a sensible and a faithful manager? Who will it be? Which of My followers will manage My affairs faithfully?" We are all managers, but Jesus wants to know who will be a *good* manager.

Before any of us raise our hands and say, "I will, I will," we had better make sure we know what the responsibilities of a good manager are. Chances are the last time you ate at a restaurant you saw a person walking around, giving direction to the hostess or the servers or the cooks. You were probably watching a manager at work. Most likely the owner was not even on the premises. In fact, the owner might have five or six restaurants around the area, or perhaps around the country. So in order for that owner to make that establishment profitable, she tries to find a man or a woman who will manage each of the restaurants for her. This is how business is run these days in hotels, gas stations, health clubs, convenience stores, and many other businesses. They are often run by managers who are hired by owners and then entrusted with the full responsibility of the day-to-day operations. Managers are in a very important position.

In this session we will try to understand what it means to be a manager and how we can be good and faithful stewards of what God has placed in our care. A very important part of being a Christian is understanding what kind of manager God wants us to be. Maybe it's necessary for us to back up one step and answer a more basic question. What is it that I, as a follower of Christ, am supposed to be managing? What has God put me in charge of? What did God turn over to my care? The specific things we will look at in this session include the secret things of God, spiritual gifts, our households, and our bodies. These are all things God has placed in our care and called us to manage in a way that is pleasing to Him.

## A WIDE ANGLE VIEW

**1** Have you ever been managed by a great manager? What made that manager great?

**2** Why is it so critical for a business, church, or any organization to have effective managers?

## A BIBLICAL PORTRAIT

Read Luke 12:42–48

**3** How does Jesus portray the faithful manager and the unfaithful manager?

*What consequences do each of the managers face for the choices they make?*

*How do you feel when you read this parable? What kind of annual review would the owner give you as manager?*

## SHARPENING THE FOCUS

Read Snapshot "The Secret Things of God"

### THE SECRET THINGS OF GOD

We have received the challenge to be managers of the secret things of God. You say, "What does that mean?" In 1 Corinthians 4:1–2 Paul says, "So then, men ought to regard us as servants of Christ and as those entrusted with the secret things of God. Now it is required that those who have been given a trust must prove faithful." Paul felt the full weight of responsibility to be a good manager of the truths of the Christian faith. Paul realized that God's plan for saving sinners, growing up believers, transforming a troubled world, and building a healthy church had been entrusted to believers. He knew we must be very careful in how he handled each of these. We have been called to manage or steward the very truth of God.

4 What are some of the "secret things of God" we need to manage faithfully?

*What can we do to grow in our knowledge of these "secret things" and effectively manage them?*

Read Snapshot "Spiritual Gifts"

### SPIRITUAL GIFTS

We have been called to steward our spiritual gifts. In 1 Peter 4:10 we read "Each one should use whatever gift he has received to serve others, faithfully administering God's grace in its various forms." Peter is saying that God has done something as a symbol of His grace and His love for you. The minute you entered the family of God, without your even knowing it, God decided sovereignly to endow you with at least one spiritual ability that would give you the capacity to be of great service to other people in the family of God. Some of you were given teaching gifts, preaching gifts, hospitality gifts, counseling gifts, pastoring gifts, shepherding gifts, leadership gifts, mercy gifts, giving gifts, administration gifts, and all kinds of other gifts. They were given as entrustments, as God's investment in you.

God says, "You don't own that gift. It's My gift. But I'm endowing you with it, and I'm asking you to steward it. I'm asking you to manage it." And what does God mean when He asks you to manage your spiritual gift? He means, first of all, to identify it. Make sure you know what it is. But then what? Develop it and sharpen it. And finally, He calls you to use it for His glory.

5 What is one of your spiritual gifts, and how are you using it as a good and faithful manager?

*What are you doing to develop and sharpen this spiritual gift?*

Read Snapshot "Households"

### HOUSEHOLDS

We are called to be managers of our households. Paul addresses this in 1 Timothy 3:4–5. Although the strict context of this passage refers primarily to elders and deacons, it implies a responsibility all believers have. Our own households include property and people, values and activities. We are all called to help manage what God has placed in our care.

**6** How can we effectively manage the material things God has put in our care?

**7** How can we effectively manage those people in our home that God has placed in our care?

Read Snapshot "Our Bodies"

### OUR BODIES

Let's say you were given a divine eviction notice and had to vacate your body for five years. Suppose that before you left you had to choose someone else to manage your body during your absence. This person would be responsible to feed your body, exercise it, condition it, care for it, rest it, and manage it while you are gone. Then, after the five years are over, you come back and take up residency in your body again.

We really are called to be managers of our bodies. The apostle Paul addressed this topic in 1 Corinthians 6:19–20. The key part of the text says, "You are not your own; you were bought at a price. Therefore, honor God with your body." Our bodies are the dwelling place of God's Holy Spirit. We are called to manage them well.

**8** If you had to leave your body in the care of someone else for five years, who would you leave it with and why?

*Would you leave your body in the care of someone just like you? Why or why not?*

## 9

What practical things can you do to be a better manager of your body? Think about sleep, eating, exercise, drinking, vacations, work, and sexuality.

**PUTTING YOURSELF IN THE PICTURE**

## Management Goals

In this lesson you have reflected on four very specific areas of spiritual management. Take time this week to identify one area in which you want to grow in your commitment to being a good manager of what God has placed in your care. Find a friend to pray for you and keep you accountable to work at this goal.

# Leader's Notes

Leading a Bible discussion—especially for the first time—can make you feel both nervous and excited. If you are nervous, realize that you are in good company. Many biblical leaders, such as Moses, Joshua, and the apostle Paul, felt nervous and inadequate to lead others (see, for example, 1 Cor. 2:3). Yet God's grace was sufficient for them, just as it will be for you.

Some excitement is also natural. Your leadership is a gift to the others in the group. Keep in mind, however, that other group members also share responsibility for the group. Your role is simply to stimulate discussion by asking questions and encouraging people to respond. The suggestions listed below can help you to be an effective leader.

## Preparing to Lead

1. Ask God to help you understand and apply the passage to your own life. Unless that happens, you will not be prepared to lead others.
2. Carefully work through each question in the study guide. Meditate and reflect on the passage as you formulate your answers.
3. Familiarize yourself with the leader's notes for each session. These will help you understand the purpose of the session and will provide valuable information about the questions in the session.
4. Pray for the various members of the group. Ask God to use these sessions to make you better disciples of Jesus Christ.
5. Before the first session, make sure each person has a study guide. Encourage them to prepare beforehand for each session.

## Leading the Session

1. Begin the session on time. If people realize that the session begins on schedule, they will work harder to arrive on time.
2. At the beginning of your first time together, explain that these sessions are designed to be discussions, not lectures. Encourage everyone to participate, but realize some may be hesitant to speak during the first few sessions.
3. Don't be afraid of silence. People in the group may need time to think before responding.

4. Avoid answering your own questions. If necessary, rephrase a question until it is clearly understood. Even an eager group will quickly become passive and silent if they think the leader will do most of the talking.

5. Encourage more than one answer to each question. Ask, "What do the rest of you think?" or "Anyone else?" until several people have had a chance to respond.

6. Try to be affirming whenever possible. Let people know you appreciate their insights into the passage.

7. Never reject an answer. If it is clearly wrong, ask, "Which verse led you to that conclusion?" Or let the group handle the problem by asking them what they think about the question.

8. Avoid going off on tangents. If people wander off course, gently bring them back to the passage being considered.

9. Conclude your time together with conversational prayer. Ask God to help you apply those things that you learned in the session.

10. End on time. This will be easier if you control the pace of the discussion by not spending too much time on some questions or too little on others.

We encourage all small group leaders to use *Leading Life-Changing Small Groups* (Zondervan) by Bill Donahue while leading their group. Developed and used by Willow Creek Community Church, this guide is an excellent resource for training and equipping followers of Christ to effectively lead small groups. It includes valuable information on how to utilize fun and creative relationship-building exercises for your group; how to plan your meeting; how to share the leadership load by identifying, developing, and working with an "apprentice leader"; and how to find creative ways to do group prayer. In addition, the book includes material and tips on handling potential conflicts and difficult personalities, forming group covenants, inviting new members, improving listening skills, studying the Bible, and much more. Using *Leading Life-Changing Small Groups* will help you create a group that members love to be a part of.

Now let's discuss the different elements of this small group study guide and how to use them for the session portion of your group meeting.

## THE BIG PICTURE

Each session will begin with a short story or overview of the session theme. This is called "The Big Picture" because it introduces the central theme of the session. You will need to read this section as a group or have group members read it on their own before discussion begins. Here are three ways you can approach this section of the small group session:

- As the group leader, read this section out loud for the whole group and then move into the questions in the next section, "A Wide Angle View." (You might read the first week, but then use the other two options below to encourage group involvement.)
- Ask a group member to volunteer to read this section for the group. This allows another group member to participate. It is best to ask someone in advance to give them time to read over the section before reading it to the group. It is also good to ask someone to volunteer, and not to assign this task. Some people do not feel comfortable reading in front of a group. After a group member has read this section out loud, move into the discussion questions.
- Allow time at the beginning of the group for each person to read this section silently. If you do this, be sure to allow enough time for everyone to finish reading so they can think about what they've read and be ready for meaningful discussion.

## A WIDE ANGLE VIEW

This section includes one or more questions that move the group into a general discussion of the session topic. These questions are designed to help group members begin discussing the topic in an open and honest manner. Once the topic of the session has been established, move on to the Bible passage for the session.

## A BIBLICAL PORTRAIT

This portion of the session includes a Scripture reading and one or more questions that help group members see how the theme of the session is rooted and based in biblical teaching. The Scripture reading can be handled just like "The Big Picture" section: You can read it for the group, have a group member read it, or allow time for silent reading. Make sure everyone has a Bible or that you have Bibles available for those who need them. Once you have read the passage, ask the question(s) in this section so that group members can dig into the truth of the Bible.

## SHARPENING THE FOCUS

The majority of the discussion questions for the session are in this section. These questions are practical and help group members apply biblical teaching to their daily lives.

## SNAPSHOTS

The "Snapshots" in each session help prepare group members for discussion. These anecdotes give additional insight to the topic being discussed. Each "Snapshot" should be read at a designated point in the session. This is clearly marked in the session as well as in the leader's notes. Again, follow the same format as you do with "The Big Picture" section and the "Biblical Portrait" section: Either you read the anecdote, have a group member volunteer to read, or provide time for silent reading. However you approach this section, you will find these anecdotes very helpful in triggering lively dialogue and moving discussion in a meaningful direction.

## PUTTING YOURSELF IN THE PICTURE

Here's where you roll up your sleeves and put the truth into action. This portion is very practical and action-oriented. At the end of each session there will be suggestions for one or two ways group members can put what they've just learned into practice. Review the action goals at the end of each session and challenge group members to work on one or more of them in the coming week.

You will find follow-up questions for the "Putting Yourself in the Picture" section at the beginning of the next week's session. Starting with the second week, there will be time set aside at the beginning of the session to look back and talk about how you have tried to apply God's Word in your life since your last time together.

## PRAYER

You will want to open and close your small group with a time of prayer. Occasionally, there will be specific direction within a session for how you can do this. Most of the time, however, you will need to decide the best place to stop and pray. You may want to pray or have a group member volunteer to begin the session with a prayer. Or you might want to read "The Big Picture" and discuss the "Wide Angle View" questions before opening in prayer. In some cases, it might be best to open in prayer after you have read the Bible passage. You need to decide where you feel an opening prayer best fits for your group.

When opening in prayer, think in terms of the session theme and pray for group members (including yourself) to be responsive to the truth of Scripture and the working of the

Holy Spirit. If you have seekers in your group (people investi-
gating Christianity but not yet believers) be sensitive to your
expectations for group prayer. Seekers may not yet be ready
to take part in group prayer.

Be sure to close your group with a time of prayer as well. One
option is for you to pray for the entire group. Or you might
allow time for group members to offer audible prayers that
others can agree with in their hearts. Another approach
would be to allow a time of silence for one-on-one prayers
with God and then to close this time with a simple "Amen."

# SONS AND DAUGHTERS

*John 1:12; Galatians 4:4–7;*
*1 John 3:1*

## INTRODUCTION

This session focuses on the new position we have as sons and daughters of God. This is a session which can evoke deep joy as well as profound sorrow. Any time we discuss God as our heavenly Father, we bring up issues of our earthly fathers. The natural parallels drawn between earthly fathers and our heavenly Father can be helpful or a real hinderance, depending on the kind of experiences we had with our earthly father.

Take time to pray for each group member. Ask God the Father to help each person to have a greater understanding of His love and affection by the time the session is finished. Pray for honest interaction and sensitive listening in the group.

## THE BIG PICTURE

Take time to read this introduction with the group. There are suggestions for how this can be done in the beginning of this leader's section.

## A WIDE ANGLE VIEW

**Question One** This question can open the door for a whole spectrum of interaction. Some will have wonderful and tender stories of a loving and caring father. Others will have stories that may surprise or even shock group members. If your group is fairly new, the dialogue might stay more on the surface. If you have been together long enough to build trust in the group, there could be substantial and deep disclosure. Be ready to spend some time on this question if the discussion moves to a deep level.

If a group member tells about some experience that was deeply wounding, pause and pray for the strength, healing, and presence of God to touch that person's life and heart.

## A BIBLICAL PORTRAIT

**Read John 1:12; Galatians 4:4–7; and 1 John 3:1**

### SHARPENING THE FOCUS

**Read Snapshot "The Father's Adoption"
before Question 3**

**Questions Three & Four** One helpful idea here would be to
think about the implications of an earthly adoption. When a
child is adopted, what rights and prerogatives does that child
receive? When we realize we have been adopted by God, we
begin to see the implications of our being sons and daughters.
We have been chosen by God to be His precious children.
One unique element of being adopted by God is the heavenly
implication. We are now heirs of the riches of heaven. Take
time to discuss the heavenly treasures that await all who are
sons and daughters of God.

**Read Snapshot "The Father's Affection"
before Question 5**

**Questions Five & Six** If we are going to live as fully devoted
followers of Christ, we must learn to walk in His love. Our
heavenly Father wants us to receive His love and to share it
freely with others. Take time as a group to share various ways
we experience the Father's love. Also encourage creative and
practical discussion on how we can share the affection and
love of the Father with others.

**Read Snapshot "The Father's Authority"
before Question 7**

**Questions Seven & Eight** Sons and daughters of loving
fathers are eager to find out how they can please their Father.
They want to hear His voice and to heed it. They want to follow His path, address His agenda, pursue His plans, and submit themselves wholly to His authority. Invite group members to submit to God's fatherly authority in their lives.

**Question Nine** One final item on the beauty of the doctrine
of adoption is that if each of us are sons and daughters of God
the Father, that makes us brothers and sisters! That's who we
are to one another. I can't tell you how many times I have
heard the words, "In so many respects the Willow Creek family, the people of this church, are the only family I have."
Those words always resound in my ears. That's true for many
of us for one reason or another. We're in a mobile, fragmented

society, and for some of us the believers we know are the only real family we have.

That's why God the Father, when He gave instruction through the writers of Scripture, said so tenderly, "Please, please, sons and daughters, treat each other like brothers and sisters. Be brotherly toward each other. Be sisterly toward each other. Don't be cruel. Don't be self- centered. Don't be insensitive. Encourage one another and share with one another, tell the truth to one another. Warn and admonish one another. Pray for one another. Love and treasure one another."

## CLOSING PRAYER

You may want to use the following prayer in a closing time of commitment: "Father, I want to live in an awareness every day of Your affection toward me. I want to feel safe and secure and loved and treasured. But I also want to live under Your authority, because a loving Father knows what's best for His children. So now, Father, I yield myself to you. I want to act as a good son or daughter would act. I want to trust Your guidance, Your judgment, Your leadership. Take my life, Father. Use it for Your glory."

## PUTTING YOURSELF IN THE PICTURE

Let the group members know you will be providing time at the beginning of the next session for them to discuss how they have put their faith into action. Let them tell about how they have acted on one of the two options above. However, don't limit their interaction to these two options. They may have put themselves into the picture in some other way as a result of your study. Allow for honest and open communication.

Also, be clear that there will not be any kind of a "test" or forced reporting. All you are going to do is allow time for people to volunteer to talk about how they have applied what they learned in your last session. Some group members will feel pressured if they think you are going to make everyone report on how they acted on these action goals. You don't want anyone to skip the next group because they are afraid of having to say they did not follow-up on what they learned from the prior session. The key is to provide a place for honest communication without creating pressure and fear of being embarrassed.

Every session from this point on will open with a look back at the "Putting Yourself in the Picture" section of the previous session.

# SAINTS

## *Ephesians 1:1, 18; 2:19; 3:8; 4:11–13; 5:3; 6:18*

### INTRODUCTION

This session focuses on the new position we have as saints. Many followers of Christ can understand being a child of God, an ambassador, a servant, a manager, and many other new identities. However, they may have a hard time seeing themselves as saints. In some cases this is due to a church background which may have a very strong sense of saints as those who have been formally acknowledged by the church. Others may struggle with this identity because they know the condition of their own heart and life is not very "saintly." The fact is, few of us get up in the morning, look in the mirror, and see the face of a person we would call a saint.

This session will help group members on three levels. First, it will help them understand the biblical declaration that all believers are saints. Second, it will help them reflect on their feelings of what it means to be a saint. Third, it will give opportunity for group members to grow in attitudes and actions which reflect this new identity they have in Christ.

### THE BIG PICTURE

Take time to read this introduction with the group. There are suggestions for how this can be done in the beginning of this leader's section

### A WIDE ANGLE VIEW

**Question One** Allow time for discussion of various perspectives. You are not looking for a right or wrong answer here. Simply allow group members to share about their view of what a saint looks like. Some may have very strong feelings because of their upbringing and church background.

**Question Two** Most people have had a few individuals in their lives who have lived what we might call a "saintly" life. Allow a time for group members to tell about those people who have impacted their lives through their example and faith. Although all believers are made saints through the work of Jesus on the cross, there is nothing wrong with holding a special admiration and appreciation for those followers of Christ who have led exemplary lives of faith.

## A Biblical Portrait

### Read Ephesians 1:1, 1:18, 2:19, 3:8, 4:11–13, 5:3, and 6:18

(In the New International Version of the Bible, the word saint is sometimes translated "God's people" or "God's holy people." It will be helpful for you to point this out if you are reading from the NIV.)

**Question Three** Why does Paul use the term "saint" so freely and frequently in many of his other letters? I think it's because he wanted every single believer to get used to the idea that in God's eyes each and every believer is a saint. You see, that is the miracle of the transforming work of Jesus Christ. He makes saints out of sinners.

All who have trusted in the death and resurrection of Jesus Christ as their only hope of forgiveness and their only hope for heaven, are saints. We may not dress like "saints" or always act like "saints," but we are saints! These passages will begin to clarify what the apostle Paul meant when he called all believers saints.

## Sharpening the Focus

### Read Snapshot "Your Position as a Saint" before Question 4

**Question Four** It helps us to accept the truth of our position as saints when we realize how we have become saints. God is the one who brought about this dramatic and eternal change in your position. You simply acknowledged the truth about your sinfulness, acknowledged that Christ is the Savior, and that you wanted to trust Him for the forgiveness of your sins.

At the moment of salvation, God lifted you from the camp of the condemned and placed you all the way over on the other side in the fellowship of the forgiven. Your position changed. Permanently! And then God said, "Now because of your new position, because now you are Mine forever, set apart in My family, set apart for My affection, set apart for My favor, you have been cleansed from sin, filled with My spirit, clothed with the righteousness of Christ, and sealed for a home in heaven forever.

We have been set apart by God. That's what the term saints really means. Set apart. The people who live in the camp of the condemned are a part of the mass of humanity that self-ishly lives unto themselves and who will pay for it in eternity. People who have trusted Christ are moved all the way over by God—to the fellowship of the forgiven—and they're set apart from the mass of humanity. They are called out, set apart, to give worship to God and to serve fellow saints. They're set apart to get organized in churches and to reach those outside the family. They're set apart to be infused with a spiritual gift. They're set apart to be given a home in heaven some day.

Why do we have a hard time seeing ourselves as saints? I think almost every single believer spends more time bemoaning the fact that he doesn't behave like a saint than he does worshiping God for his position as a saint. I know I do. I can think about my position as a saint and dwell on that a little bit, and in thirty seconds I'm saying, "But I didn't talk like one at the dinner table, and I didn't treat my daughter like one yes-terday before school when she didn't get ready in time. I didn't treat a staff member like I should have today and I lost my self-control . . . a saint wouldn't do that."

**Question Five** Isn't it time that some of us focus more atten-tion on the wonder of our position instead of always jumping to the frustrations and failures of our practice? Imagine a father who has always wanted a son and for some reason couldn't have one. Finally, he adopts a twelve-year-old boy. He wants to love that little guy and to bring him into the fami-ly and let him know he is really a part of the family. He show-ers love and affection on the boy. Can you imagine the father's frustration as he puts the boy to bed and he says, "I'm so glad you're my son. I'm so glad you're legally adopted into this family and you're mine." And then to have the son say, "But sir, I left my bike out last night and I know I didn't take the garbage out, and I said I'd do the dishes and I didn't, and. . . ." That Father would say, "Right now, I'm talking about how wonderful it is for you to be in my family and for you to be a part of my very own home and my dreams." And the kid says, "Yeah, but my bike, Dad, you know, my bike." What the father longs for is love and a relationship with his boy.

I'll bet there have been many times when God your heavenly Father, in your times of prayer and devotion, was saying to you, "Celebrate your position. You're mine. You're a saint. You've been set apart. You're in the fellowship of the forgiven. And you're Mine forever. We'll talk about your foul ups later. Let's celebrate your new status now."

The primary way that I'm trying to do this in my own life is in the morning when I journal and I write out my prayers. I try to spend more and more time reflecting on and worshiping God for the fact that I have been miraculously lifted out of the camp of the condemned and tenderly placed into the fellowship of the forgiven. I try to dwell on that before I digress into self-examination and critique. I stay right there and feast on my position and thank God for it. I'm saved. I'm secure in His love. I'm heaven bound. I'm a son. I have access to the Father. I have brothers and sisters. I have the Holy Spirit.

**Read Snapshot "The Life of a Saint" before Question 6**

**Question Six** As the group discusses this question, allow for varied answers. Let this be a brainstorming session of those things that can and should mark our lives as saints. By the end of this time of sharing, most, if not all, of the group members will be identifying areas in which they need to grow in their walk with Jesus.

**Question Seven** When you don't act like a saint, remember what camp you're in. I don't know how many Christians commit a serious or a not-so-serious sin, and the first thing that strikes them is, *I am no longer in the fellowship of the forgiven. I have reverted all the way back to the camp of the condemned. I'm not saved any more. I'm not heaven bound anymore. Oh no, this tragedy has struck, so now what?* When this kind of thinking comes, it's so important to have a strong grip on your new position. Once you are in the fellowship of the forgiven, you're in there to stay. And no one, John 10 says, can take you out of that camp. No one. So, when you don't act like a saint, remember that you're still in the camp of the forgiven and you have been forgiven once and for all positionally. You can be sure that Jesus Christ will apply His cleansing blood to the foul-ups in your daily behavior if you ask Him to. This is true for you and true for other followers of Christ. Walk in God's forgiveness and share it freely with others.

## PUTTING YOURSELF IN THE PICTURE

Challenge group members to take time in the coming week to use part or all of this application section as an opportunity for continued growth.

# SOLDIERS

## *Ephesians 6:10–18*

### INTRODUCTION

This session focuses on the new position we have as soldiers. God calls us to serve Him in the spiritual battles we will face each day. The central question asked in this session is, "What kind of soldier will I be?" God desires for us to be "Just Say The Word" soldiers who are ready to follow Him into battle no matter what the cost.

The battles we will face are real. Our enemy is well-equipped, deceptive, and dangerous. Group members need to begin thinking in military terms. This session will help participants see themselves as soldiers in God's army.

### THE BIG PICTURE

Take time to read this introduction with the group. There are suggestions for how this can be done in the beginning of the leader's section.

### A BIBLICAL PORTRAIT

**Read Ephesians 6:10–18**

**Question Two** You may want to read Matthew 8:5–13 in preparation for this discussion. It recounts the story of Jesus and the centurion. It may even be helpful to read this as a small group within the context of this part of your discussion.

If I'm not mistaken, this centurion is the only man in all of Scripture who Jesus marveled at. Why was Jesus astonished at this Roman soldier? This soldier simply made a straightforward request on behalf of his servant. Jesus offered to come and heal him. But the centurion lets Jesus know He does not have to come to his house, all He has to do is say the word and he knows the servant will be healed.

You see, here's the fascinating point. This soldier understands all about authority and submission as it pertains to the military. He says, "Jesus I understand some basics. You see, I have soldiers above me, and I have soldiers below me. And all of us know that without discipline and authority and submission, there would be chaos in the camp." And then, without batting an eyelash he says, "And I know that You, Jesus, are in authority over me, over my servant, and over my servant's illness. You are the absolute authority in this world. We are all submissive to You right now, so just say the word." And Jesus was amazed.

In verse 10 Jesus said, "I have not found anyone in Israel with such great faith." So Jesus healed the soldier's servant, long distance, that very hour. I think, as Jesus walked away, He might have been thinking, "Oh, give Me a few hundred soldiers like this soldier in My army and watch out world. Give me a whole unit of men and women who understand submission, authority, lordship, leadership, and faith."

What is some of the military language used in the Bible and by followers of Christ? The man who had the single greatest impact on casting the vision for Willow Creek's ministry over twenty years ago is Dr. Gilbert Bilezikian. He often uses military language when discussing strategies and ministry. When a ministry is moving forward, instead of saying it's moving forward, he says it's defeating the enemy. When we talk about the possibility of starting satellite churches, he talks about establishing a beach head. He talks about sending supplies and reinforcements to fellowships that are struggling and losing ground. And when we as a church feel we're under attack by Satan, he talks about launching a counteroffense and getting sweet revenge.

Obviously, the apostle Paul had similar feelings as he penned the famous passage about spiritual warfare in Ephesians 6.

## SHARPENING THE FOCUS

### Read Snapshot "Weekend Warriors" before Question 3

**Question Four** The weekend warrior rut is easy to fall into. As soldiers of Jesus Christ, discuss the impact of those who don't take the battle seriously. Because there are many people like this in the church, be ready for some lively discussion. However, remember, the goal is not to name or put down those who are struggling in the battle but to strategize how you can help them get back on the front line.

### Read Snapshot "Soldiers Gone AWOL" before Question 5

**Question Six** As you enter this discussion, remember that some AWOL soldiers have pulled away from the church and the battle because they have been wounded, sometimes even by "friendly fire" from their own camp. Some have been beat up and hurt by other believers or churches that have not expressed the love and care of Jesus. Strategize together how you can help bring these brothers and sisters back into fellowship. Who are specific people you need to reach out to?

**Read Snapshot "'Just Say the Word' Soldiers" before Question 7**

**Question Eight** You may want to look at 2 Timothy 2:3. The apostle Paul says to young Timothy, "Endure hardship with us like a good soldier of Christ Jesus." One of the costs of being a good soldier is to be willing to suffer hardship for a worthy cause. Without question, most of the great stories of courage come from the lives of soldiers who suffered unbelievable hardships during times of war. Paul, the seasoned soldier of Christ, writes a letter to young Timothy who could be compared to a buck private. He warns Timothy that good soldiers of Jesus Christ will face hardship in the battle. And Paul instructs Timothy not only to expect hardship, but to endure it.

Simply put, soldiering always involves suffering. Some will suffer to a greater degree than others, but all soldiers face suffering. Don't think for one minute that you're going to face a different course than all the Christians throughout history have faced. Jesus said, "You're going to have to deny yourself, take up your cross daily, and follow me."

Not many sermons, admittedly, are given on this subject. Not many teachers enjoy teaching this part of the faith because people at large are pleasure-seeking, comfort-intensive beings. Tell a seeker or a weak, half-hearted believer that hardships and satanic resistance and attacks will cause heartache and headaches and hassles, and watch how many go AWOL. But Paul takes his chances and he says, "Let's just let the truth be known. Soldiers will face suffering. This is war. The stakes are sky high. We're fighting over the destiny of human beings who matter to God." Jesus, our leader, willingly bled to death to gain the ultimate victory over the enemy, and He expects us to pay a price for the victories that we gain over the Evil One as well.

**Question Nine** There is a part of Christianity that is intensely private. There are moments when you are reading your Bible and it says, "Do this and that," and you know you're not doing this and that, and you face a moment of truth. What kind of soldier are you? Are you ready to say, "Just say the Word," no matter what the cost?

There are moments when you're going about your business and the Lord gives you a clear call to serve or reach out to a specific person. In these moments of truth, what kind of soldier are you? It's in those moments that the battles are won and lost. No matter how many Sunday mornings services you attend and how many Bible studies you join, you still need to say, "Just say the word" in those critical moments of daily life. You can memorize Scripture. You can pray elaborate prayers. You can carry a big Bible. You can smile Christian smiles and put Christian bumper stickers on your car. But the battles are won or lost in those moments of truth when you are sensing the leading of God and you have to say, "What kind of soldier am I at this moment? Am I one who understands authority and submission? Am I ready to say yes, no matter what the cost?"

**Question Ten** Close your time together by identifying specific tactics and strategies you can use as individuals and a group to be "Just Say the Word" soldiers in God's service. Share specific battlefields and your assessment of how the fight is going. No soldier can make it on his own. Discuss specific ways you can support and reinforce each other in the battle.

## PUTTING YOURSELF IN THE PICTURE

Challenge group members to take time in the coming week to use part or all of this application section as an opportunity for continued growth.

# AMBASSADORS

## 2 Corinthians 5:16–20

### INTRODUCTION

This session focuses on our new identity as ambassadors. When we become followers of Christ, we are called to be His ambassadors. We are the messengers who bring the Good News of Jesus to lost people. The goal in this session is to identify various kinds of ambassadors and seek to be effective kingdom ambassadors.

### THE BIG PICTURE

Take time to read this introduction with the group. There are suggestions for how this can be done in the beginning of this leader's section.

### A WIDE ANGLE VIEW

**Question One** Here are five qualities you may want to think about and discuss:

First, if I were going to look for the ideal ambassador I would want someone with wisdom and discernment. I would want a mature person who was seasoned, who knew how to act, and who knew what to say and what not to say in certain circumstances. I would look for a wise person who had a sort of sixth sense for doing and saying right things.

Second, this might surprise you a little bit, but I would look for someone who had a quality that I call winsomeness. You know, in a highly charged setting, a winsome individual can build lots of bridges of understanding and defuse a lot of anger. A winsome person is someone who is relational, courteous, a good listener, and who has a good sense of humor. Someone who is hospitable, conversational, and likeable. I think a wise, winsome person would be a good candidate for an ambassador.

Third, I would look for someone who is knowledgeable. Someone who is completely familiar with the history and values of the other people and someone who is completely familiar with the history and values of our people. For an ambassador, a lack of knowledge can prove to be deadly.

Fourth, I would look for an articulate communicator. Someone who expresses himself or herself accurately, concisely, yet with an ease and a confidence. An ambassador should be an excellent communicator if at all possible.

And finally, I would look for someone who had a personal interest and passion as opposed to finding someone who is merely looking for a secure government job. I'd want someone who just loved the country and the people and longed to see them reconciled, communicating with each other, trading with each other, traveling back and forth. I'd look for someone with a vested interest, someone with a kind of internal drive that would go beyond the job description.

Provide time for your group members to write their own want ad. You may also want to have group members volunteer to read their want ads.

## A Biblical Portrait

Read 2 Corinthians 5:16–20

### Sharpening the Focus

**Read Snapshot "The Anonymous Ambassador" before Question 3**

**Question Three** An anonymous ambassador can reside in a foreign land for twenty years and never advance the cause of reconciliation one bit, which seems like a colossal waste of an opportunity, doesn't it? Why is he an ambassador if he locks himself in the embassy? He's an anonymous ambassador. The silence of an anonymous ambassador can keep people from finding the truth of Jesus. Their refusal to get out of the embassy makes reconciliation almost impossible.

You see, anonymous ambassadors are oblivious to Spirit-orchestrated opportunities to mark the lives of unbelievers. Anonymous ambassadors are hiding out in the embassy. They're not praying for opportunities to mix with citizens, and they don't recognize them when they come.

**Read Snapshot "The Obnoxious Ambassador" before Question 4**

**Question Four** There are some people who could be called obnoxious kingdom ambassadors. Admittedly, obnoxious ambassadors can do some good. Some people are reconciled to God through obnoxious ambassadors. But more harm is done than anyone can calculate, because large numbers of people end up feeling more alienated than ever before. They end up further from God, and angrier at Him, than if there had been no ambassador at all. You see, anonymous ambassadors don't do much, but obnoxious ambassadors do the kind of things we wish they wouldn't do. For instance, they often barge into private areas with or without opportunities being opened up by the Spirit.

Isn't it time that some of the obnoxious ambassadors in the kingdom cool their jets a little bit and realize that causing increased alienation among seekers is a serious and potentially damning ministry? Isn't it time that obnoxious ambassadors stop their buttonholing and their overzealous, high-pressure tactics, and be reminded that most people would rather be escorted carefully to the place of reconciliation instead of intimidated? Isn't it time for God's ambassadors to learn to reach out to seekers with tactics that will draw them in rather than drive them farther away?

**Read Snapshot "The Effective Ambassador"
before Question 5**

**Question Five** Some time ago on a flight from New York to Chicago, I ended up sitting next to a man who lived quite near our church. When I told him what my name was he recognized it and said, "You're mixed up with that Willow Creek Community Church." And I said, "So I am." I asked him what he had heard about the church and he said, "Oh mostly good things, really." And then he let it be known to me he was not interested in God, and doubly not interested in church. So I silently prayed, "Lord what would you have me do? Here's a man that matters to you. He needs to be reconciled to God, and I'm an ambassador. What should I do?"

I thought that if he wouldn't talk about God or church, maybe he would talk about something else. I discovered he was willing to talk about business, which we discussed for forty-five minutes, which then led into a conversation about burnout. Throughout the course of the discussion he told me he hadn't taken a vacation in eight years. I asked him about the toll that had taken on his wife and children, and he started to get very personal. I said, "Would you allow me to send you a couple books on burnout and how you can avoid the ravages of that kind of thing?" He said, "I would really like that." And so I sent him two Christian books that speak to the issue and are laced with references to the love of Christ.

I felt affirmed by the Holy Spirit that I did the right thing in that situation. If I had done less than that, I would have been copping out. If I had done more than that, I believe I would have caused further alienation. An effective kingdom ambassador looks for opportunities, prays for opportunities, and when he senses that God is providing them he says, "Oh God, give me wisdom, right here and right now. How far should I take this? Should I challenge this person? Should I just love him? Lead me, Holy Spirit, and I'll follow." And that's where the adventure of being an ambassador really comes into play.

**Question Six** Take a moment to read Colossians 4:5. An effective kingdom ambassador must receive and apply God's Wisdom. Paul says, "Be wise in the way you act toward outsiders; make the most of every opportunity." Be wise in your relationships with outsiders. Seize and make the most of Spirit-produced opportunities.

Wisdom comes in many forms. We need to look in the Bible for our primary source of wisdom. God has given us His Book to help us walk on the paths of wisdom. Daily reading of the Bible is a key to growing in wisdom. Also, we gain wisdom when we walk with the wise. There are many people with whom we can spend time and draw from their wisdom. We need to work at being with those who will influence us in God's wisdom.

**Question Seven** An effective kingdom ambassador needs to be winsome. Look at Colossians 4:6. It says, "Let your conversation be always full of grace, seasoned with salt, so that you may know how to answer everyone." Interesting, isn't it? It says if you really want to build rapport with outsiders, if you want to be an effective, winsome, kingdom ambassador, then let the general flow of your conversation be gracious, but seasoned with salt. See the balance again? An anonymous ambassador speaks all grace. An obnoxious ambassador speaks all salt. An effective ambassador speaks with grace, seasoned with salt. A winsome ambassador learns how to respond, the verse says, to each person. Being winsome involves understanding the nature of the person you are trying to reconcile to God and trying to relate to that person positively and creatively.

Being winsome involves a willingness to become genuinely interested in whatever interests the one you are trying to influence. It involves being thoughtful and servant-like and humble. And being winsome involves being real, letting someone see that you have the same kinds of struggles and problems that everybody else has.

**Question Eight** Effective kingdom ambassadors are knowledgeable of the land, the values, and the people they're trying
to influence. They are also knowledgeable about the land, the
values, and the people they represent. Both are essential. We
must know what's going on in the world and what is happening in the lives of the people we're trying to influence. There
are subject areas I find to be critical as I seek to be an ambassador. These are nonnegotiables if I want to be a knowledgeable, effective kingdom ambassador.

I have to be absolutely up-to-date on all current events. When
I talk to men and women in the marketplace, one of the first
conversations is current events . . . who's covering what up,
what the stock market did. I need to know what's going on in
the world around me. So I read the paper and four or five mag-
azines each week. I also watch the evening news and listen to
the news station on the radio, because I need to be able to
have instant recall of those kinds of tidbits of information that
establish bridges of communication. I have to be knowledgeable about what's going on in the world in which these people
are living.

I also find it critical to be aware of financial matters. If I am
going to be in regular contact with seekers, I need to be aware
of those things that matter to them. Finances come up often in
conversations, and I need to know about what is happening in
this part of life. Athletics are also important. For me, and
many Christian men, being up on athletics is critical if we are
going to communicate with seekers. In short, we need to be
tuned in to the things seekers are thinking about. If we are
going to talk to them about our world, we need to be able to
discuss their world with intelligence. This means working at
being aware of what is happening in the world around us.

**Question Nine** Effective ambassadors must know the values
of the land in which they are living. They must also be knowledgeable concerning matters of the heavenly kingdom they
represent. 2 Timothy 2:15 says, "Do your best to present
yourself to God as one approved, a workman who does not
need to be ashamed and who correctly handles the word of
truth." 1 Peter 3:15 says, "But in your hearts set apart Christ as
Lord. Always be prepared to give an answer to everyone who
asks you to give the reason for the hope that you have. But do
this with gentleness and respect." We need to be knowledgeable about our world. I think every believer should have a little library of key books and tapes to serve as resource material
for questions that might arise. Are you in touch with culture
enough to speak intelligently to people in it about what's

going on? And are you confident enough about what you know about kingdom matters that you can talk effectively with people about that?

**Question Ten** Effective kingdom ambassadors are greatly aided if they can communicate clearly. You know, if you're wise and winsome and knowledgeable, and if you are praying for opportunities to reconcile people to God to what Christ has done on the cross, the Holy Spirit will open up opportunities. He will. Sooner or later you're going to have one of those moments when a seeker will say, "Just tell it to me. How can I be reconciled to God?" When one of those moments come, you'd better be able to answer the question articulately and concisely.

## PUTTING YOURSELF IN THE PICTURE

Challenge group members to take time in the coming week to use part or all of this application section as an opportunity for continued growth.

# FRIENDS

## *John 15:9–17*

### INTRODUCTION

If we can grasp the significance of this message, watch out. In this session, we're looking at the place where Jesus announces yet another dimension to our new identities. He says, "I want you to all know that when I look at you as my followers, I see you as being My friends, My personal, close, trusted friends. Yes, you are sons and daughters and saints and soldiers and ambassadors, but let it be known, you've got a friend." And, He says, "It's Me."

This session is a great chance to rejoice in the gift of God's friendship extended through Jesus. It is also a chance to develop that friendship by learning how we can do our part to grow in our relationship with Jesus. As you prepare to lead this session, ask yourself a few honest questions. Do you feel His friendship? Do you really? Do you rejoice in the fact that you've got a friend in Christ? Do you enjoy the friendship that's been extended to you? Or is it difficult for you to accept and appropriate? Don't be surprised if you find yourself having to admit that it is difficult for you to accept and appropriate the friendship of Jesus. Many Christians have a hard time getting their mind around this concept. As you lead this session, realize some of your group members may struggle with this concept. Pray for Jesus to help you understand His friendship and to communicate it effectively to your group members.

### THE BIG PICTURE

Take time to read this introduction with the group. There are suggestions for how this can be done in the beginning of the leader's section.

### A BIBLICAL PORTRAIT

**Read John 15:9–17**

### SHARPENING THE FOCUS

**Question Three** The first and greatest proof of Jesus' friendship is found in John 15:13, "Greater love has no one than this, that he lay down his life for his friends." We know through history He's done exactly that. Verses 14 and 15 are tied together and provide the second proof of His friendship. He says, "Friends respect each others' values. I know you'll respect My values and you'll obey Me. I know that. I respect you. I know you'll respect Me." Then Jesus explains that because He views us as friends, He has not requested blind obedience from us. He has not demanded mindless acquiescence to His commands. What Jesus is saying is that often times a slave owner will bark out orders and say in effect, "Obey and don't ask why. Yours is not to reason why. Don't question me, don't ask for explanations, don't second guess me, just do it."

He says in verse 15, "I want you to know something, friend. I'm not holding out on you. I'm not holding back vital information My Father would like to convey to you. I'm not playing any games with you. You're My friends. I'm giving you all the pertinent information that's been given to Me. For all things I have heard from My father, I have made known to you, because you're My friends." It's His way of saying, "I'd like for you to rest in this truth. I'd like for you to rejoice in it. I'd like for it to impact the way you live." In summary, He says, "I want all of you people to know, you've got a friend."

**Read Snapshot "Increased Time Together" before Question 5**

**Question Five** The same relational principle for human friendships applies to improving our friendship with Jesus. Each individual believer must come to grips with how much time they need to spend with the Lord each day in order to keep that all-important relationship healthy and growing. It varies from Christian to Christian. And what actually occurs during those fellowship times with the Lord varies from believer to believer as well. But let it be known, the quality of your friendship with Jesus depends in large part on your willingness to invest time in your schedule for the expressed purpose of fellowshipping with Him.

I want to share with you one of the greatest mistakes I made earlier in my ministry. I made a one-to-one equation of improving my relationship with Christ by solely increasing my service to Him. I thought if I just got more active, if I attended more things and got more involved, then I would improve my friendship with Christ. I remember a few brothers saying to me, "Bill, you've missed it. God isn't so much looking for your frenzied activity, He would just like some fellowship with you. He'd really like it if you'd just sit at His feet, talk to Him. Tell Him how you think and feel about Him, listen to Him, meditate on Him." You might know the story about Mary and Martha in the New Testament. Martha is busy, scurrying all over, doing all the domestic activities. Mary is sitting at the feet of the Savior. Jesus says, "There's one smart sister here. She's just sitting at my feet." There's a time for religious activity, but not to the exclusion of fellowship. You may want to read Luke 10:38–42 and reflect on the story of these two sisters.

How do you fellowship with the Lord? There's a variety of ways. Through Bible study, meditation, journaling, praying, worshiping, listening. James 4:8 says, "Come near to God and he will come near to you." In other words, spend time with God and you will feel closer to Him. The friendship will grow. If you really want to discover how wonderful it is to be friends with Jesus, you need to make slots throughout your day into which you can schedule time to be in fellowship with Him. It may seem awkward at first but it will seem natural after that, and after awhile you will not be able to live without it.

**Read Snapshot "Removing Barriers" before Question 6**

**Question Six** When there are barriers between us and Jesus, they are all on our side. He removed the barriers on His side at the cross. However, we develop some barriers with Him, don't we? Sometimes we put up a barrier when we begin to doubt His wisdom. When we look at the mountain instead of the sufficiency of the mountain mover. When we question His guidance. When we rebel at some of His requests. When we refuse to repent even though we've wronged Him. As those barriers come into focus, they have to be dealt with or the friendship factor will come to a standstill in your relationship with Jesus.

One of the reasons every single believer should be at the communion table every time is because the communion celebration is a kind of spiritual tune-up. It's the taking of a spiritual inventory that provides us with an opportunity to identify if there are any barriers in our relationship with the Lord or with brothers and sisters. Then you can talk honestly to the Lord about them in the hopes of removing these barriers as soon as possible.

One reason why I write out my prayers of confession every day is because I want to work through any barriers in my relationship with the Lord. I just say, "Lord what's standing in the way? What am I doing wrong? What am I refusing to do? What am I rebelling about? What is it in my life?" Aren't we supposed to be "Just Say The Word" soldiers? Aren't we supposed to be the kind of people who say, "Oh Lord, whatever's a barrier . . . if there is fear, disobedience, a lack of trust, whatever it is, oh Lord, I want to be a righteous person. I confess this sin. Forgive it. I want to be done with it so I can have a barrier-free relationship"?

You may want to allow group members to spend about five to ten minutes alone with the Lord confessing anything that has become a barrier in their friendship with Him. Encourage them to get alone, find a place where they can talk to Jesus, and say, "Lord I know there's a barrier here. I know what the blockage is, and I want to tell you, I want to confess it as a sin, and I want for it to be removed." If you allow time for this, when you come back together, spend a moment praying for the group and thanking God for His forgiveness. You may also want to read 1 John 1:9 before this exercise.

**Read Snapshot "Serving Jesus" before Question 7**

**Question Seven** Jesus has served each one of us and has proved His friendship beyond the shadow of a doubt. Greater love has no one than this, that He laid down His life for His friends (John 15:13). He's made the ultimate demonstration of His servanthood on the cross. He delights in His continued servanthood to you. He protects you, provides for you, answers your prayers, empowers you, guides you, and forgives you. As you turn and serve Him, your relationship with Him will deepen. It really will.

Your service to Jesus—if motivated by love and gratitude—is one of the absolutely essential building blocks in your relationship to Him. You will feel the friendship factor with Jesus more when you're serving Him. The more you serve Him, the closer you will feel to Him. The more you love Him, the more the relationship will grow. Surely the church benefits from your service to Jesus, but the ultimate motivation behind your service should be a love for Jesus and a desire to improve your relationship with Him through mutual servanthood: His serving of you, and your serving of Him.

Any believer who has served Christ faithfully for any period of time will tell you that some of the most precious moments in their friendship with Jesus came in the trenches of servanthood. If you're not serving Jesus, you're impairing your friendship with Him. Find a place to serve. Talk with your church leaders and find out where you can serve Jesus in a way that is consistent with your gifts and abilities. Find a place to serve Jesus and let it deepen your friendship with Him.

**Read Snapshot "Saying 'I Love You'" before Question 8**

**Question Eight** I have made it a practice in my home to be an absolute fanatic when it comes to saying "I love you." We take in boarders now and then, and I'm sure it takes them awhile to get used to how many hundreds of times we say "I love you" around our house. I say to Lynne, "I love you, babe, I love you." My daughter, Shauna, said to me one day, "I love you, buster." We say it sternly, musically, dramatically, even boringly. That verbal affirmation reinforces how precious those relationships really are. I try to do the same thing with some close friends. And when others say those words to me it has a powerful effect on me.

God has said those words to us in His own way, hasn't He? Over and over again, in a variety of ways, Jesus affirmed His love to His followers and to us. Over and over He says, "I love you, I love you friend." Do you have any idea how He would like to hear you say, "Well I love You too. I love You Jesus." And isn't that really the essence of worship? Isn't that when an individual believer throughout the day just says, "I love You too, Jesus." Do you have any idea what that means to Him?

That is why corporate worship is such a profoundly meaningful activity to God. To have all of the core of the church together and say, "Us too. We know You love us Lord, but we just have to say that we love You too!" The more you worship and return the love of Christ, there's a deepening in the friendship that occurs.

I'd just like to encourage you all again, throughout your day, as you write out your prayers, if you sing them, if you paint them, no matter how you say them, just say those words often, "I love You too, Lord." Remember, He initiates the love. All you have to do is say, "I love You, too."

## PUTTING YOURSELF IN THE PICTURE

Challenge group members to take time in the coming week to use part or all of this application section as an opportunity for continued growth.

# MANAGERS

## *Luke 12:42–48*

### INTRODUCTION

The final new identity we will look at in this series is that of being a manager. God has placed many things in our care and has called us to faithfully manage them. In this session we will focus on four central areas of stewardship. We have been given the responsibility of managing the secret things of God, our spiritual gifts, our households (both relationships and material things), and our bodies. In this session you will identify these central areas of personal management and grapple with how you can grow in being faithful managers of all God has entrusted to you.

### THE BIG PICTURE

Take time to read this introduction with the group. There are suggestions for how this can be done in the beginning of the leader's section.

### A WIDE ANGLE VIEW

**Question Two** A close friend of mine has the title of general manager of a very large company. His responsibilities are enormous. The owner has entrusted him with tremendous amount of responsibility and opportunity. Often managers have to assemble and organize the efforts of a staff. They have to provide the service or make the product. They have to watch expenses. They have to earn profits. They have to troubleshoot. They have to give five-year, ten-year, fifteen-year plans. For all intensive purposes, the manager is running that particular establishment on behalf of the owner who entrusted him with this great responsibility.

I think if we spent a little time pondering the matter, we would arrive at a fresh appreciation of how important it is for an owner to select and to employ the right manager. He's got to find a sensible, honest, faithful, conscientious, communicative manager. The right manager can render valuable service to the owner and help his endeavor to succeed. The wrong manager can do a ton of damage to an owner and can even make a viable venture fail.

## A BIBLICAL PORTRAIT

**Read Luke 12:42–48**

## SHARPENING THE FOCUS

**Read Snapshot "The Secret Things of God"
before Question 4**

**Question Four** The apostle Paul says, "Woe be to anybody who distorts the truth of God's word. You cannot be a faithful steward if you go around distorting that which you are called to manage." Good stewards don't distort the truth. He also says, "Don't take the truth of God lightly" or "Woe unto those who know the truth but refuse to share it with other people." Paul said to a church he was leaving, "I never did shrink back from declaring to you the whole council of God. I managed all of these truths and presented them to you courageously. I didn't save some fine print. I didn't hold back the tough stuff."

Paul knew that God had entrusted him with truth that could change people's lives and eternities. He said, "I've been given this truth. Now I have to manage it carefully. I have to teach it. I have to apply it to my life. I have to spread it out worldwide. I can't shrink back from declaring it to anyone who will listen." And you don't have to be a great Bible student to figure out that Paul was a good student of the secret things of God. Paul took beatings, physical beatings, rather than compromise biblical truth. He was imprisoned rather than staying silent about it. He taught the truth passionately, lived the truth dynamically, and spread the truth all over the known world. Paul was a good steward, a faithful manager of the secret things of God.

We have to ask ourselves, what kind of managers are we with the truth we have in our possession? The information in the Bible can transform people's lives and eternities. It's the only book that has that power. What are you doing with this truth? Are you a good steward of it? Are you managing these truths wisely, courageously, effectively, and without apology?

Think about Jesus at the time of His ascension. He has gathered all His disciples around Him and is going to return to the Father. When you think about it, all that He was leaving behind was a message and a few friends. He had shed His own blood as a payment that would allow lost people to find God's forgiveness in what He did for them on the cross. Now Jesus was taking this whole message of salvation and entrusting it to eleven tattered men. If they would be good stewards, then all of the rest of people throughout history would have a chance to be redeemed. But if they were careless and unfaithful managers, the priceless treasure would be squandered. It was all a question of stewardship. Let's be thankful for their faithful managing and learn to walk in their footsteps.

**Read Snapshot "Spiritual Gifts" before Question 5**

**Question Five** Faithful managers of spiritual gifts please the owner to no end. It gives God so much pleasure to see His people using and stretching and developing their spiritual gifts. He says, "That's what I gave them to you for." All of you have gifts. The question is, what kind of manager are you? I pray that you're being a careful steward of your gifts. Are you taking this call seriously, developing your gift and bearing much fruit?

You may want to ask your small group what would happen in your church if, instead of preaching a sermon, the pastor simply said, "This morning we are going to have every church member stand and say their name, spiritual gift, and how they are using this gift in service to God"? Would you have a lively and joyous time celebrating the giftedness and ministry of God's people, or would it be a time of uncomfortable silence?

Every church member should be using the spiritual gifts God has given them in such a way that they would be ready and able to tell others about their ministry and service in God's kingdom.

**Read Snapshot "Households" before Question 6**

**Question Six** Managing your own household means you are to be a conscientious, sensible, and faithful steward of your property. That includes your money and all the material goods you have. All of this belongs to God, but its yours to manage. It includes the management of your shelter—your home or apartment—and your vehicles. It also includes furniture, bikes, lawn mowers, and everything else. God is the ultimate owner, but He asks us to take care of these things. He wants you to manage them wisely.

So I say to you, on the authority of God's Word, vacuum His carpet, keep His lawn nice, wash His car, and manage His money wisely. Poor stewardship of property is not only an affront to God but it is also very costly. It contributes to a consumptive lifestyle when we don't manage our possessions wisely. They're God's possessions, but you're asked to take care of them.

**Question Seven** Our management of people is even more important than our management of things. Spouses are entrustments from God. You know what Jesus says to husbands? "Be a faithful manager of your wife." And wives, He says to you, "Be a faithful manager of your husband. Take care of your husband." Children are also an entrustment from God. We are to steward our spouse and our children carefully, conscientiously, in a God-honoring fashion.

**Read Snapshot "Our Bodies" before Question 9**

**Question Nine** God says to manage your body carefully. Part of that means not putting garbage in it. Vast numbers of Christ followers put wrong foods into their bodies. There are those who neglect exercise. There are those who smoke and who drink in a destructive fashion. There are people who, in general, just abuse that which God has asked them to carefully and conscientiously manage. I wonder how we're going to give an account of that kind of management. Are we going to say, "Well you know, I managed your mysteries, my spiritual gifts, the household, but I took a pass on managing my body?" I hope not. Let's be good managers of *every* area God has entrusted to us.

## PUTTING YOURSELF IN THE PICTURE

Challenge group members to take time in the coming week to use part or all of this application section as an opportunity for continued growth.

# ADDITIONAL WILLOW CREEK RESOURCES

### Small Group Resources

*Leading Life-Changing Small Groups*, by Bill Donahue

The Walking with God Series, by Don Cousins and Judson Poling

### Evangelism Resources

*Becoming a Contagious Christian* (book), by Bill Hybels and Mark Mittelberg

*Becoming a Contagious Christian* (training course), by Mark Mittelberg, Lee Strobel, and Bill Hybels

*Inside the Mind of Unchurched Harry and Mary*, by Lee Strobel

*Inside the Soul of a New Generation,* by Tim Celek and Dieter Zander, with Patrick Kampert

*The Journey: A Bible for Seeking God and Understanding Life*

*What Jesus Would Say,* by Lee Strobel

### Spiritual Gifts and Ministry

*Network* (training course), by Bruce Bugbee, Don Cousins, and Bill Hybels

*What You Do Best,* by Bruce Bugbee

### Marriage & Parenting

*Fit to Be Tied*, by Bill and Lynne Hybels

### Authenticity

*Honest to God?*, by Bill Hybels

*Descending into Greatness*, by Bill Hybels

### Ministry Resources

*Rediscovering Church*, by Bill Hybels

*The Source*, compiled by Scott Dyer, introduction by Nancy Beach

*Christianity 101*, by Gilbert Bilezikian

All of these resources are published in association with Zondervan Publishing House.

# Discover your place of ministry in God's Kingdom

## What You Do Best
### *In the Body of Christ*
#### Bruce Bugbee

As believers, we are called to be involved in some ministry arena. The question is: "Where should I serve?" In *What You Do Best,* Bruce Bugbee helps you identify your God-given passion, spiritual gifts, and personal style. He then shows how, together, these three aspects point to your unique role and purpose in the body of Christ. Once you learn what God wants you to do, you will experience more enthusiasm, greater joy, and real significance in your life and your personal ministry role.

Softcover: 0-310-49431-1

# Get your whole church plugged into ministry for the Kingdom

## Network
### *The Right People... In the Right Places...*
### *For the Right Reasons...*
#### Bruce Bugbee, Don Cousins, and Bill Hybels

If you are responsible for recruiting and staffing at your church, you need *Network,* a revolutionary, biblically based program for helping people discover their passion, spiritual gifts, and personal style—and leading them into a meaningful ministry role for service in the church. The clear and detailed Leader's Guide, along with the overheads and powerful videos make this Gold Medallion Award-winning course easy to lead in any setting—from small group to Sunday school to large-group seminars.

Kit includes:
- Video 1: Network Drama Vignettes
- Video 2: Network Vision and Consultant Training
- Overhead Masters
- 1 Leader's Guide
- 1 Participant's Guide

Curriculum Kit: 0-310-20046-6
Participant's Guide also available separately: 0-310-41231-5

*Look for both* What You Do Best *and* Network *at your local Christian bookstore.*

## ZondervanPublishingHouse
*Grand Rapids, Michigan*

*A Division of* HarperCollins*Publishers*

### WILLOW CREEK RESOURCES
*Helping People Become Fully Devoted to Christ*

*This resource was created to serve you.*

It is just one of many ministry tools that are part of the Willow Creek Resources® line, published by the Willow Creek Association together with Zondervan Publishing House. The Willow Creek Association was created in 1992 to serve a rapidly growing number of churches from all across the denominational spectrum that are committed to helping unchurched people become devoted followers of Christ.

The vision of the Willow Creek Association is to help churches better relate God's solutions to the needs of seekers and believers. Here are some of the ways it does that:

- **Church Leadership Conferences**—3¹/₂-day events, generally held at Willow Creek Community Church in South Barrington, IL, that are being used by God to help church leaders find new and innovative ways to fulfill and expand their ministries.
- **The Leadership Summit**—a once-a-year event designed to increase the leadership effectiveness of pastors, ministry staff, and volunteer church leaders.
- **Willow Creek Resources®**—to provide churches with a trusted channel of ministry resources in areas of leadership, evangelism, spiritual gifts, small groups, drama, contemporary music, and more. For more information, call Willow Creek Resources® at 800/876-7335. Outside the U.S. call 610/532-1249.
- **WCA Monthly Newsletter**—to inform you of the latest trends, events, news, and resources.
- **The Exchange**—to assist churches in recruiting key staff for ministry positions.
- **The Church Associates Directory**—to keep you in touch with over 1000 other WCA member churches.

For conference and membership information please write or call:

**Willow Creek Association**
**P.O. Box 3188**
**Barrington, IL 60011-3188**
**(847) 765-0070**